SURVIVAL ENGLISH

English Through Conversations

Book 1A

SECOND EDITION

Lee Mosteller

Bobbi Paul
San Diego Community Colleges

Illustrated by Jesse Gonzales

PRENTICE HALL / REGENTS

Acquisitions editor: *Nancy Leonhardt*
Electronic production/interior design: *Louise B. Capuano*
Cover design: *Marianne Frasco*
Pre-press buyer/scheduler: *Ray Keating*
Manufacturing buyer: *Lori Bulwin*

Printed in the United States of America

10   9

ISBN 0-13-016593-X

Contents

Preface

This workbook has been designed by teachers of beginning ESL students. It is aimed towards students who have some degree of literacy and does not address preliterate skills. To be successful with this book, students should have a small oral vocabulary and a knowledge of our alphabet.

The main objective of *Survival English* is to teach the most basic functional English patterns to these students. The teaching consists of many small steps that are simple, direct, and repetitive. Because of this, a few of the dialogues will not be conversationally functional. However, the book will provide a vocabulary and structure background in which new knowledge can be integrated.

Theoretically we agree that beginning students should have generous time to develop listening skills before being expected to produce language. However, the need exists to teach literacy as soon as possible along with oral skills, and as adults, these students want to read and write immediately.

Included in each unit is a variety of exercises to reinforce the oral patterns and to teach listening, speaking, reading, and writing. Reading and writing are introduced after the student has mastered oral patterns. This book is based on the theory that students learn to speak English by listening, speaking, reading, and writing, in that order.

OBJECTIVES

1. To teach the most basic functional language patterns in survival situations.

2. To teach language patterns and vocabulary in a systematic and controlled manner.

3. To develop reading and writing skills based on what the student can produce orally.

4. To provide survival information and coping skills necessary for adult living.

ACKNOWLEDGMENTS

Our special thanks to Gretchen Bitterlin, ESL Chairperson, San Diego Community Colleges, for her encouragement and suggestions.

SURVIVAL ENGLISH

1 PERSONAL ID

Essential Vocabulary

1. good morning
how are you
I'm fine
thank you
thanks
afternoon
evening

2. is
she
busy
she's
they
they're
happy
tired
hot
cold
sad
angry

3. am
he

4. isn't
aren't
no

5. not

6. what's
her
name
Ann Lee
his
Bob Jones
first
last

7. your
my
spell that
please
middle
maiden

8. address
Main Street
telephone number
social security number

9. (review)

10. city
state
country
zip code
what

11. from
Mexico
Carbo

12. old
birth date
it's
year
month
January
February
March
April
May
June

July
August
September
October
November
December

13. married
widowed
husband
died

14. single
divorced

A. Good morning.
How are you?

B. I'm fine, thank you.
How are you?

A. Fine, thanks.

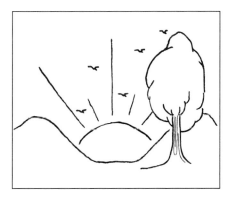

1. Good morning.

2. Good afternoon.

3. Good evening.

1.   I

2.   we

3.   he

4.   you

5.   she

6.   they

1. She's busy.   2. They're fine.

3. He's tired.   4. He's hot.

5. She's cold.   6. He's angry.

7. They're sad.   8. He's happy.

A. How is she?
B. She's busy.
A. How are they?
B. They're fine.

Match

1. fine

2. busy

3. tired

4. hot

5. cold

6. happy

7. sad

8. angry

How	are	you they	?	I'm They're	fine.
	is	he she		He's She's	

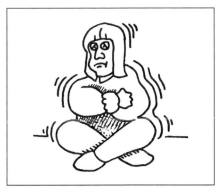

1. How is she?

_____ cold.

2. How is he?

_____ tired.

3. How are they?

_____ fine.

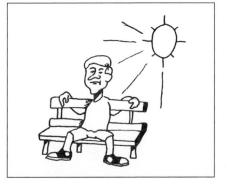

4. How is he?

_____ hot.

1. How is she?

She's _____ .

2. How are they?

They're _____ .

3. How is he?

He's _____ .

4. How is he?

He's _____ .

I'm They're	fine.
He's She's	

1. How is he? _____ _____ .

2. How are they? _____ _____ .

3. How are you? _____ _____ .

4. How is she? _____ _____ .

5. How are they? _____ _____ .

6. How is he? _____ _____ .

7. How are you? _____ _____ .

8. How is she? _____ _____ .

A. Are you busy?

B. Yes, I am.

A. Is he tired?

B. Yes, he is.

1. Are you busy?

Yes, _____ am.

2. Is he tired?

Yes, _____ is.

3. Are they happy?

Yes, _____ are.

Yes,	I	am.
	he she	is.
	they	are.

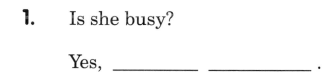

1. Is she busy?

Yes, _____ _____ .

2. Is he tired?

Yes, _____ _____ .

3. Are they sad?

Yes, _____ _____ .

4. Are you busy?

Yes, _____ _____ .

A. Is he sad?

B. No, he isn't.

A. Are they happy?

B. No, they aren't.

1. Are they happy?

No, _____ aren't.

2. Is he sad?

No, _____ isn't.

3. Is she tired?

No, _____ isn't.

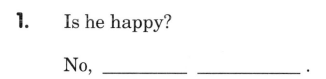

No,	he she	isn't.
	they	aren't.

1. Is he happy?

No, _____ _____ .

2. Are they sad?

No, _____ _____ .

3. Is she hot?

No, _____ _____ .

4. Is he angry?

No, _____ _____ .

1. Is he cold?

No, _____ _____.

2. Are they happy?

Yes, _____ _____.

3. Is he hot?

No, _____ _____.

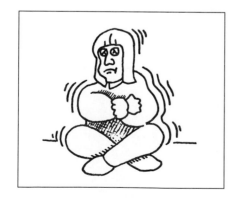

4. Is she cold?

Yes, _____ _____.

A. Are you busy?

B. No, I'm not.

---

1. Are you busy? No, I'm not.

2. Are you angry? No, I'm _____ .

3. Are you cold? No, I'm _____ .

4. Are you hot? No, _____ _____ .

5. Are you sad? _____ , _____ _____ .

6. Are you fine? Yes, I am.

7. Are you busy? Yes, I _____ .

8. Are you happy? Yes, I _____ .

9. Are you tired? Yes, _____ _____ .

10. Are you cold? _____ , _____ _____ .

Name _____

A.   What's her name?

B.   Her first name is Ann.
Her last name is Lee.

A.   What's his name?

B.   His first name is Bob.
His last name is Jones.

| **His** |
| **Her** |

1.   _____ name is Bob Jones.

2.   _____ name is Ann Lee.

Bob Jones

1. His _____ name is Bob.

His _____ name is Jones.

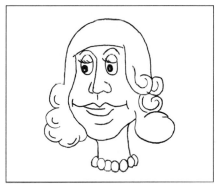

Ann Lee

2. Her _____ name is Ann.

Her _____ name is Lee.

you

3. My first name is _____ .

My last name is _____ .

A. What's your name?

B. My name is _____ .

A. What's your first name?

B. My first name is _____ .

A. Spell that.

B. _____

A. What's your last name?

B. My last name is _____ .

A. Please spell that.

B. _____

First name _____   Middle name _____

Last name _____   Maiden name _____

Last name _____

First name _____

Middle name _____

Maiden name _____

Name _____
             Last   First   Middle

Last name_____

A. What's his address?

B. 7613 Main Street.

A. What's his telephone number?

B. 560–6660.

A. What's his Social Security number?

B. 560–58–8025.

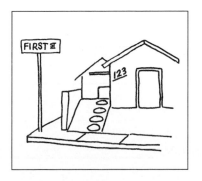

Match

1. address

2. telephone number

3. Social Security number

4. address

5. telephone number

6. address

7. Social Security number

8. telephone number

9. address

10. Social Security number

11. telephone number

12. address

1. _____   2. _____   3. _____ – _____ – _____

A. What's your address?

B. _____

A. What's your telephone number?

B. _____

A. What's your Social Security number?

B. _____

Name _____   NAME _____

Add. _____   ADDRESS _____

Tel. _____   TELEPHONE _____

Soc. Sec. No. _____ – _____ – _____   SOCIAL SECURITY _____ – _____ – _____

name _____   Name _____

address _____   Address _____

telephone _____   Telephone _____

social security _____ – _____ – _____   Social Security _____ – _____ – _____

First name _____

Bob Jones
7613 Main Street
San Diego CA 92111
U.S.A.

A. What's your address?

B. _____

A. What city?

B. _____

A. What state?

B. _____

A. What country?

B. _____

A. What's your zip code?

B. _____

address _____

city _____

state _____

zip code _____

Name	_____
	first last
Address	_____
	_____
	city state zip code
Telephone number	_____
Social Security number	_____ – _____ – _____

1. My first name is _____ .

2. My last name is _____ .

3. My address is _____ .

4. My telephone number is _____ .

5. My zip code is _____ .

6. My Social Security number is _____ – _____ – _____ .

7. My city is _____ .

8. My state is _____ .

9. My country is _____ .

Match

first name	560–58–8025
telephone number	San Diego
zip code	Jones
Social Security number	7613 Main Street
last name	92111
state	California
country	560–6660
city	U.S.A.
address	Bob

First name _____ Last name _____

Address _____

Country _____ City _____ State _____

Telephone number _____ Zip code _____

Social Security number _____ – _____ – _____

_____

last name   first name

_____

address   city   state

_____

country   zip code

_____

telephone number

A.   What country is he from?

B.   He's from Mexico.

A.   What city is he from?

B.   He's from Carbo.

A.   What country are you from?

B.   I'm from _____ .

A.   What city are you from?

B.   I'm from _____ .

_____

I'm from _____ , _____ .

Name _____

Address _____

      street   city

              _____

      state   zip code

Telephone _____

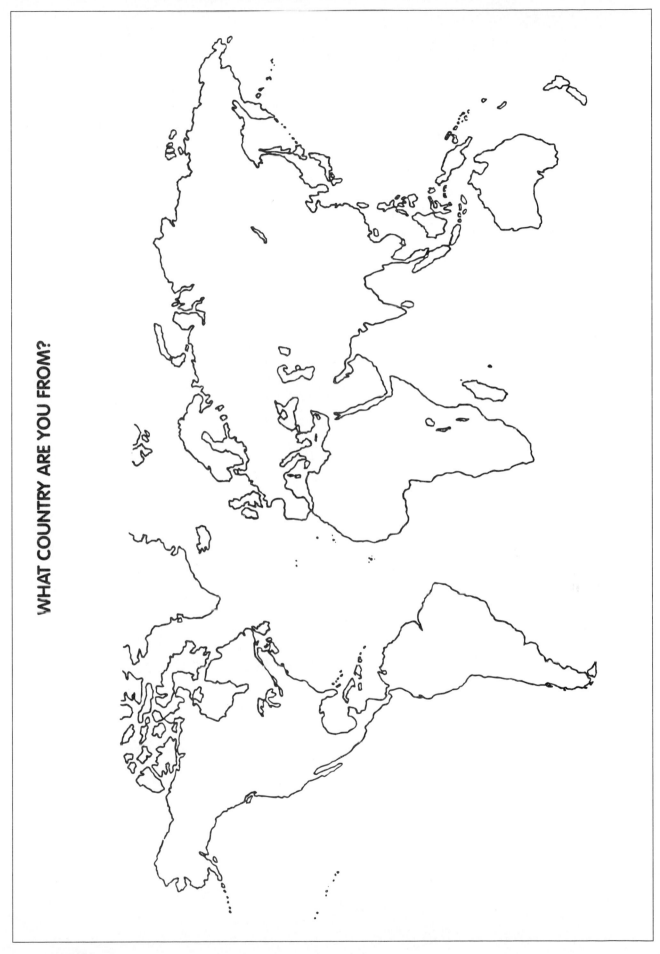

WHAT COUNTRY ARE YOU FROM?

	name	address	zip code	telephone number
1.	Bob Jones	7613 Main Street	92111	560–6660
2.	Ann Lee	6514 First Street	74920	896–7531
3.				

A. How old is Bob?

B. He's 45.

A. What's his birth date?

B. It's May 17, 1948.

A. How old are you?

B. I'm _____ .

A. What's your birthdate?

B. It's _____ ____ , 19____ .

| name | age | birth date | | |
		month	day	year
Bob Jones	45	May	17	1948

January
February
March
April
May
June
July
August
September
October
November
December

A. Is he married?

B. Yes, he is.

A. Is she married?

B. No, she isn't.
She's widowed.
Her husband died.

Yes,	he she	is.
	they	are.

No,	he she	isn't.
	they	aren't.

1. Is he married?

Yes, _____ _____ .

2. Is he widowed?

No, _____ _____ .

3. Are they married?

Yes, _____ _____ .

4. Is she widowed?

Yes, _____ _____ .

5. Is she married?

No, _____ _____ .

28

A. Is she married?

B. No, she isn't.
   She's single.

A. Is he married?

B. No, he isn't.
   He's divorced.

A. Are you married?

B. _____

1. Is she married?

   No, _____   _____ .

2. Is she single?

   Yes, _____   _____ .

3. Is he divorced?

   No, _____   _____ .

4. Is he married?

   Yes, _____   _____ .

5. Are they married?

   No, _____   _____ .

6. Are they divorced?

   Yes, _____   _____ .

Sue and Joe are married.
They're happy.
They're from Mexico.

---

1. Is Sue married?

_____ .

2. Is Joe married?

_____ .

3. Is Joe happy?

_____ .

4. Is Joe single?

_____ .

5. Is Sue single?

_____ .

6. What country are they from?

_____ .

7. Are they from Mexico?

_____ .

8. Are you married?

_____ .

	single	widowed	divorced	married
1. Ann		✔		
2. Kim			✔	
3. Lee	✔			
4. Bob				✔

1. Is Bob married?
2. Is Bob divorced?
3. Is Lee single?
4. Is Lee married?

5. Is Ann divorced?
6. Is Ann widowed?
7. Is Kim married?
8. Is Kim single?

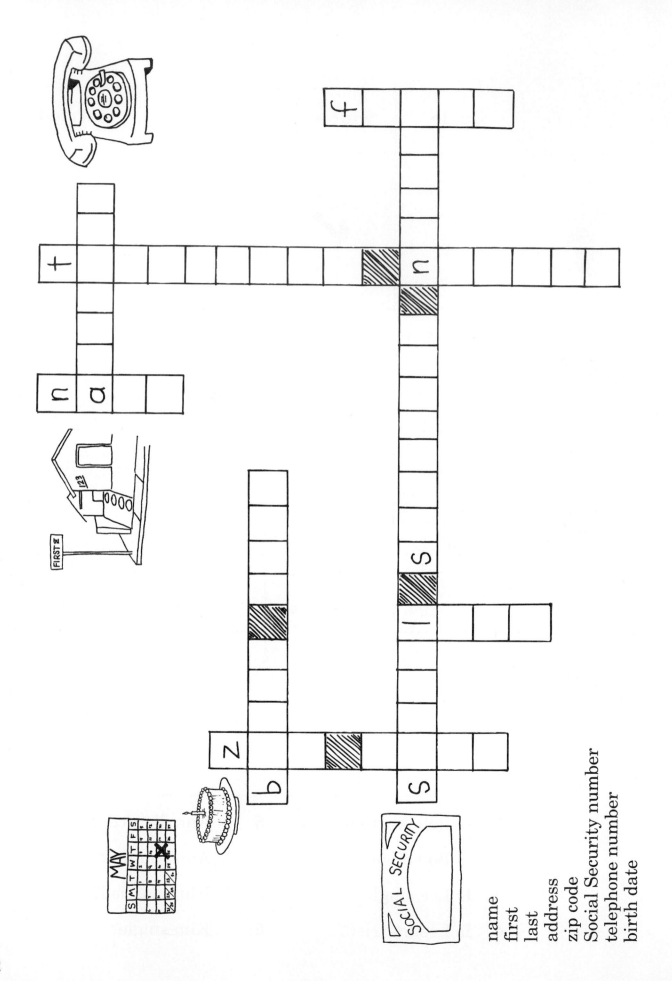

name
first
last
address
zip code
Social Security number
telephone number
birth date

2 GENERAL

Essential Vocabulary

1. where's
   the
   on
   in
   next to
   under
   over
   between
   pencil sharpener
   pen
   light
   chair
   pencil
   clock
   door
   blackboard / chalkboard
   paper
   book
   table
   window

2. stand up
   walk
   close
   open
   go out
   come in
   sit down
   read
   write

3. today
   Sunday
   Monday
   Tuesday
   Wednesday
   Thursday
   Friday
   Saturday

4. yesterday
   tomorrow
   was

5. date

   weather
   how's
   sunny
   rainy
   cloudy
   hot
   cold

7. excuse me
   time
   class
   at

8. need
penny
nickel
dime
quarter
dollar

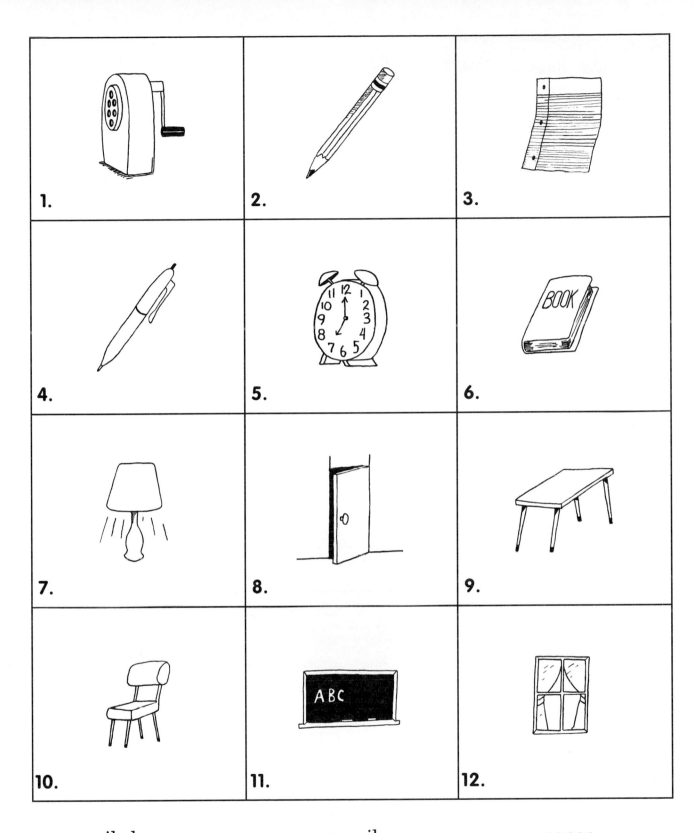

pencil sharpener	pencil	paper
pen	clock	book
light	door	table
chair	chalkboard / blackboard	window

A.   Where's the _____ ?

B.   It's | **on**
in
next to
under
over
between | the _____ .

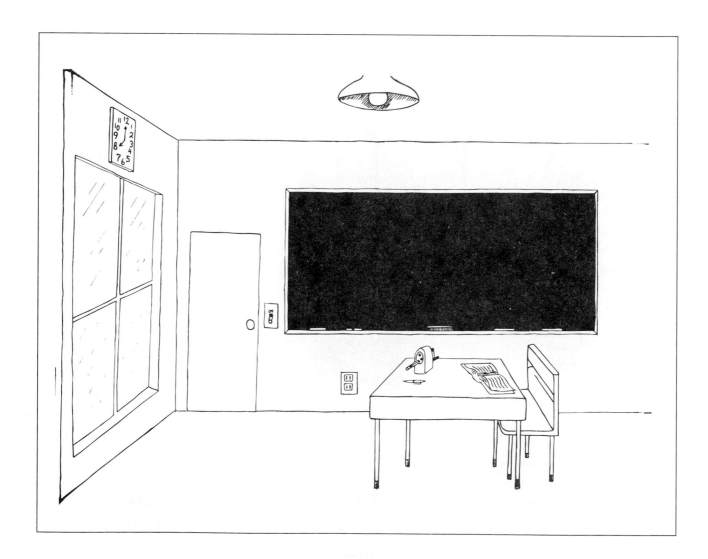

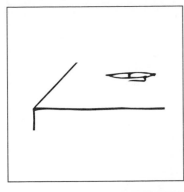

1. The pen is │ **next to** │ the table.
│ **on** │
│ **over** │

2. The clock is │ **next to** │ the window.
│ **over** │
│ **between** │

3. The pencil is │ **in** │ the pencil sharpener.
│ **on** │
│ **under** │

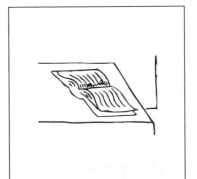

4. The door is │ **over** │ the chalkboard.
│ **between** │
│ **next to** │

5. The book is │ **on** │ the table.
│ **in** │
│ **over** │

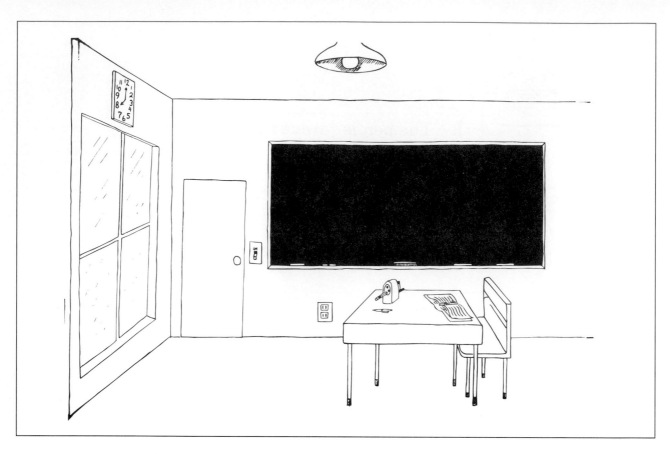

on	next to	over
in	under	between

1. The light switch is _____ the door.

2. The window is _____ the clock.

3. The pencil is _____ the pencil sharpener.

4. The book is _____ the table.

5. The light switch is _____ the chalkboard and the door.

6. The clock is _____ the window.

7. The chair is _____ the table.

8. The pencil sharpener is _____ the table.

9. The light is _____ the table.

10. The pen is _____ the pencil sharpener.

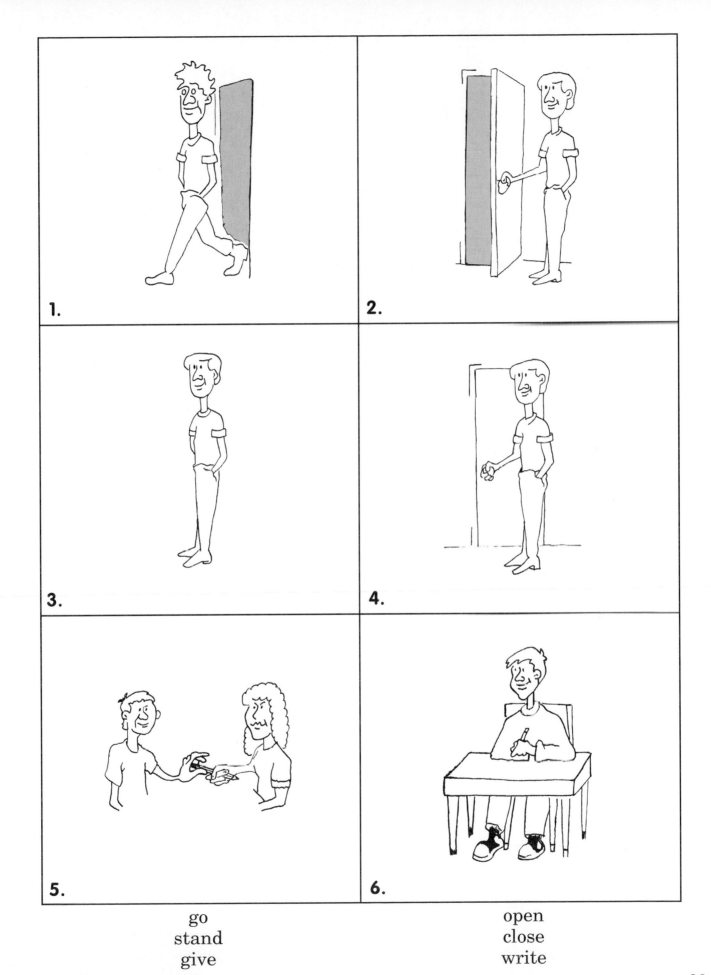

1.

2.

3.

4.

5.

go
stand
give

6.

open
close
write

1. _____ out.

2. _____ up.

3. _____ the door.

4. _____ your name.

5. _____ the door.

6. _____ him a pencil.

1. Please stand up.
2. Please go to the door.
3. Please open the door.
4. Please go out.
5. Please come in.
6. Please close the door.
7. Please go to the window.
8. Please open the window.
9. Please close the window.
10. Please walk to your chair.
11. Please sit down.
12. Please open your book.
13. Please read your book.
14. Please close your book.
15. Please write your name.
    Thank you.

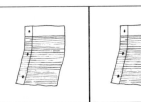

 1. _____

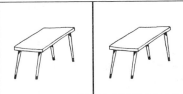 2. _____

3. _____

 4. _____

 5. _____

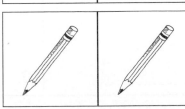 6. _____

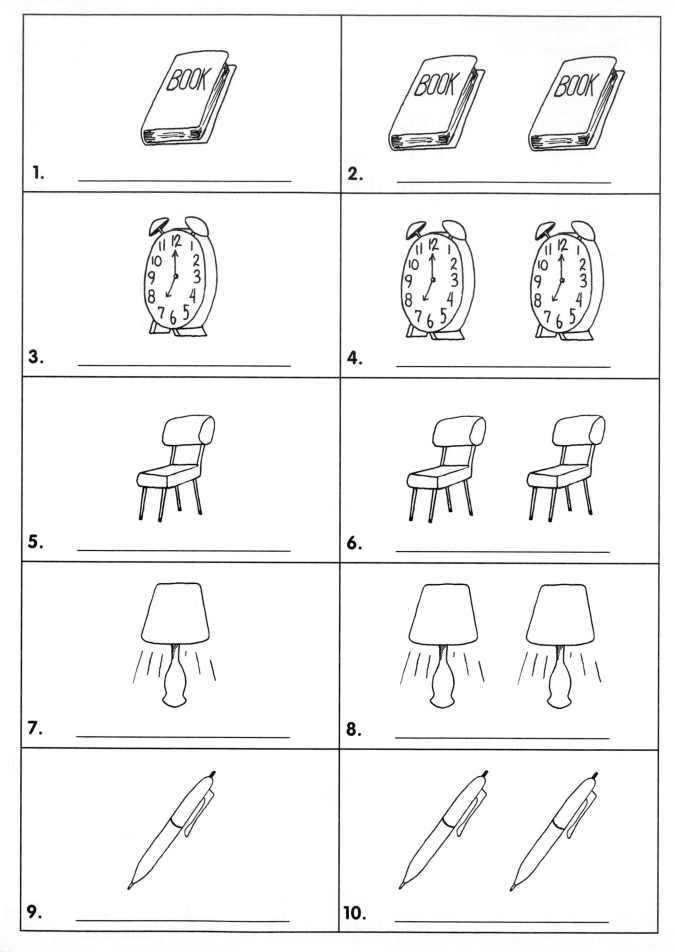

1. _____

2. _____

3. _____

4. _____

5. _____

6. _____

7. _____

8. _____

9. _____

10. _____

book
pencil sharpener
blackboard
paper
clock
table
door
light
pen
chair

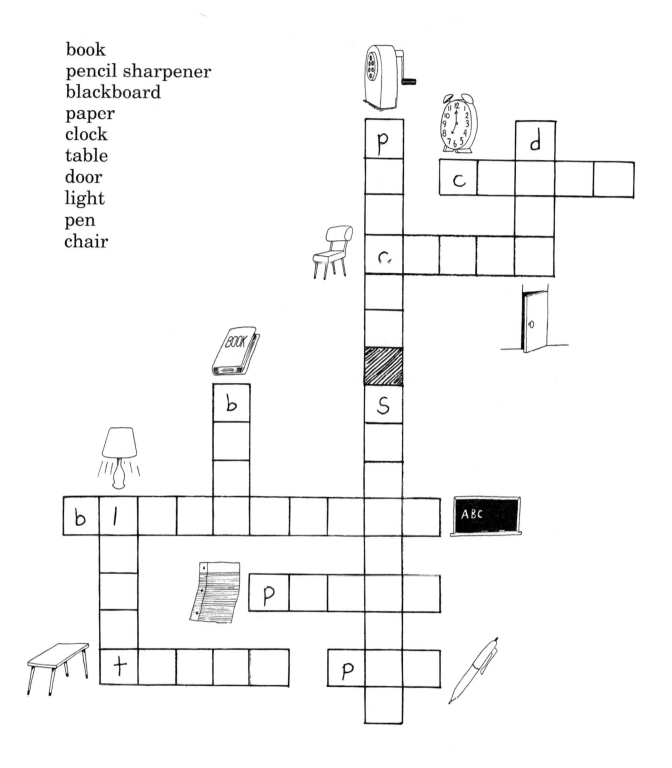

1	2	3	4	**5**	6	7	8	9	**10**
11	12	13	14	**15**	16	17	18	19	**20**
21	22	23	24	**25**	26	27	28	29	**30**
31	32	33	34	**35**	36	37	38	39	**40**
41	42	43	44	**45**	46	47	48	49	**50**
51	52	53	54	**55**	56	57	58	59	**60**
61	62	63	64	**65**	66	67	68	69	**70**
71	72	73	74	**75**	76	77	78	79	**80**
81	82	83	84	**85**	86	87	88	89	**90**
91	92	93	94	**95**	96	97	98	99	**100**

See the Teacher's Guide.

WHAT'S MISSING?

1　2　___　4　5　___　7　8　___　10

11　___　13　14　___　16　17　___　19

1　___　3　___　5　___　7　___　9　___

11　___　13　___　15　___　17　___　19

___　21　___　23　___　25　___　27　___

29　___　31　___　33　___　35　___　37

10,　20,　___　40,　50,　___　70,　80,　___　100

0	zero
1	one
2	two
3	three
4	four
5	five
6	six
7	seven
8	eight
9	nine
10	ten
11	eleven
12	twelve
13	thirteen
14	fourteen
15	fifteen
16	sixteen
17	seventeen
18	eighteen
19	nineteen
20	twenty
30	thirty
40	forty
50	fifty
60	sixty
70	seventy
80	eighty
90	ninety
100	one hundred

A.   What's today?

B.   It's _____ .

_____

1.   Sunday _____   Sun. _____

2.   Monday _____   Mon. _____

3.   Tuesday _____   Tues. _____

4.   Wednesday _____   Wed. _____

5.   Thursday _____   Thur. _____

6.   Friday _____   Fri. _____

7.   Saturday _____   Sat. _____

A. What's today?

B. It's _____ .

A. What was yesterday?

B. It was _____ .

A. What's tomorrow?

B. It's _____ .

---

1. Today is Monday.

Tomorrow is _____ .

2. Today is Wednesday.

Tomorrow is _____ .

3. Today is Friday.

Tomorrow is _____ .

4. Today is Friday.

Yesterday was _____ .

5. Today is Sunday.

Yesterday was _____ .

Address _____

A. What's the date?

B. It's _____ , _____ _____ .

---

1. January _____ Jan. _____

2. February _____ Feb. _____

3. March _____ Mar. _____

4. April _____ Apr. _____

5. May _____ May _____

6. June _____ Jun. _____

7. July _____ Jul. _____

8. August _____ Aug. _____

9. September _____ Sept. _____

10. October _____ Oct. _____

11. November _____ Nov. _____

12. December _____ Dec. _____

before	after

1. June is _____ May.

2. September is _____ August.

3. December is _____ November.

4. February is _____ January.

5. July is _____ August.

6. March is _____ May.

7. August is _____ July.

8. October is _____ November.

9. January is _____ February.

10. November is _____ December.

11. April is _____ March.

12. May is _____ June.

SEPTEMBER

Sun.	Mon.	Tues.	Wed.	Thurs.	Fri.	Sat.
		1	2	3	4	5
6	7	8	9	10	11	12
13	14	15	16	17	18	19
20	21	22	23	24	25	26
27	28	29	30			

See the Teacher's Guide.

See the Teacher's Guide.

1994

JANUARY

						1
2	3	4	5	6	7	8
9	10	11	12	13	14	15
16	17	18	19	20	21	22
23	24	25	26	27	28	29
30	31					

FEBRUARY

	1	2	3	4	5
6	7	8	9	10	11	12
13	14	15	16	17	18	19
20	21	22	23	24	25	26
27	28					

MARCH

		1	2	3	4	5
6	7	8	9	10	11	12
13	14	15	16	17	18	19
20	21	22	23	24	25	26
27	28	29	30	31		

APRIL

					1	2
3	4	5	6	7	8	9
10	11	12	13	14	15	16
17	18	19	20	21	22	23
24	25	26	27	28	29	30

MAY

1	2	3	4	5	6	7
8	9	10	11	12	13	14
15	16	17	18	19	20	21
22	23	24	25	26	27	28
29	30	31				

JUNE

			1	2	3	4
5	6	7	8	9	10	11
12	13	14	15	16	17	18
19	20	21	22	23	24	25
26	27	28	29	30		

JULY

					1	2
3	4	5	6	7	8	9
10	11	12	13	14	15	16
17	18	19	20	21	22	23
24	25	26	27	28	29	30
31						

AUGUST

	1	2	3	4	5	6
7	8	9	10	11	12	13
14	15	16	17	18	19	20
21	22	23	24	25	26	27
28	29	30	31			

SEPTEMBER

				1	2	3
4	5	6	7	8	9	10
11	12	13	14	15	16	17
18	19	20	21	22	23	24
25	26	27	28	29	30	

OCTOBER

						1
2	3	4	5	6	7	8
9	10	11	12	13	14	15
16	17	18	19	20	21	22
23	24	25	26	27	28	29
30	31					

NOVEMBER

	1	2	3	4	5
6	7	8	9	10	11	12
13	14	15	16	17	18	19
20	21	22	23	24	25	26
27	28	29	30			

DECEMBER

				1	2	3
4	5	6	7	8	9	10
11	12	13	14	15	16	17
18	19	20	21	22	23	24
25	26	27	28	29	30	31

See the Teacher's Guide.

First name _____

A. How's the weather?

B. It's rainy.

1.

2.

3.

4.

sunny   rainy
cloudy   hot / cold

1. How's the weather?

It's _____.

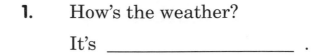

2. How's the weather?

It's _____.

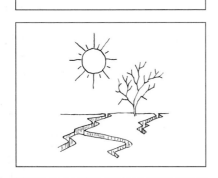

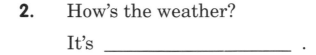

3. How's the weather?

It's _____.

4. How's the weather?

It's _____.

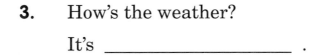

5. How's the weather?

It's _____.

6. How's the weather?

It's _____.

Last name _____

A. Excuse me. What time is it?

B. It's 8:00.

A. What time is the class?

B. It's at 8:30.

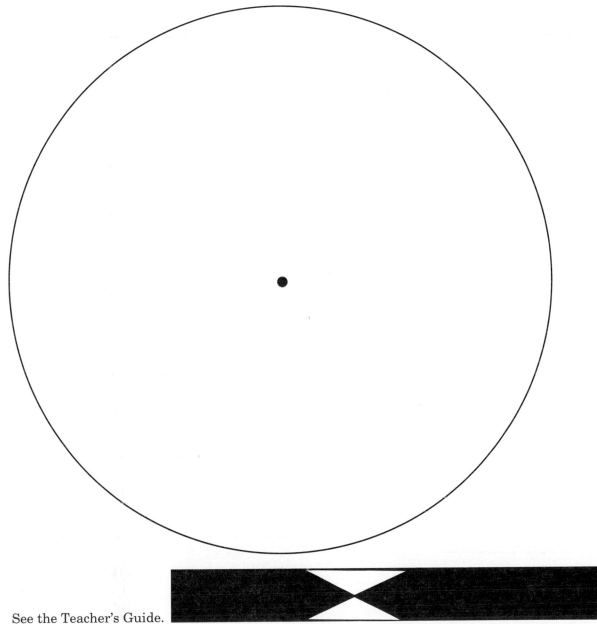

See the Teacher's Guide.

WHAT TIME IS IT?

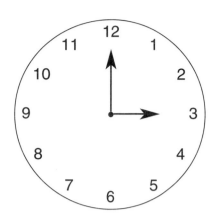

1. _____

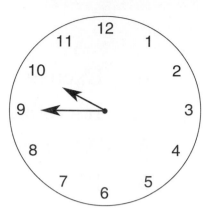

2. _____

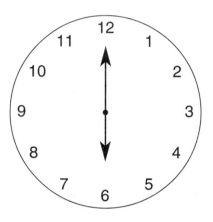

3. _____

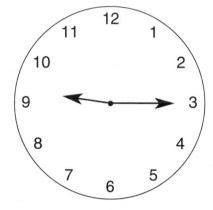

4. _____

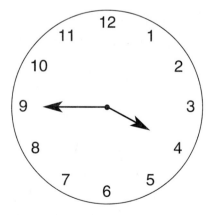

5. _____

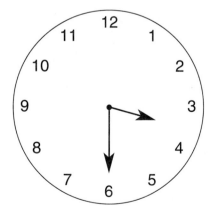

6. _____

7. _____

8. _____

9. _____

MATCH

6:15	3:00	9:15
9:45	6:00	6:45
3:45	3:30	9:30

WHAT TIME IS IT?

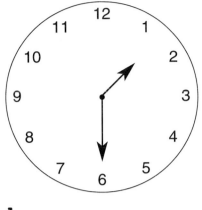 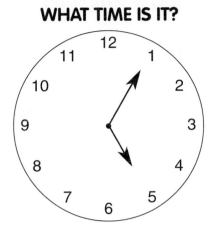 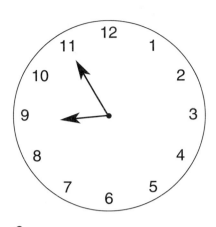

1. _____ 2. _____ 3. _____

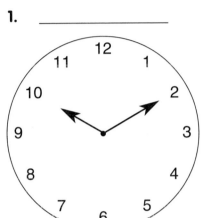 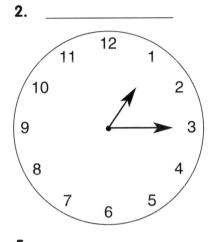 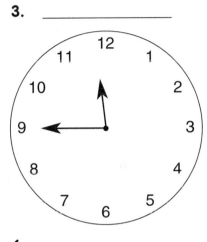

4. _____ 5. _____ 6. _____

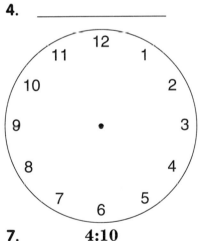 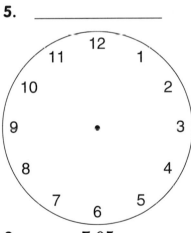 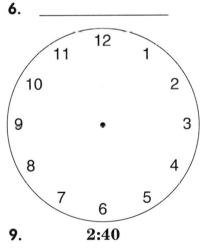

7. **4:10** 8. **7:05** 9. **2:40**

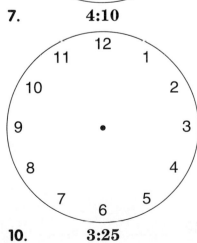 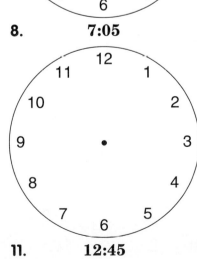 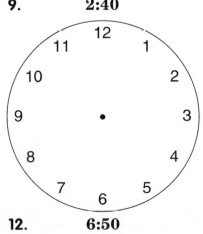

10. **3:25** 11. **12:45** 12. **6:50**

WHAT TIME IS IT?

1. _____

2. _____

3. _____

4. _____

5. _____

6. _____

7. _____

8. _____

9. _____

10. _____

11. _____

12. _____

		Free		

See the Teacher's Guide.

a	b	c	d	e
f	g	h	i	j
k	l	m	n	o
p	q	r	s	t
u	v	w	x	y
z	ch	th	sh	wh

See the Teacher's Guide.

WHAT'S MISSING?

1. a b ____ d e f ____ h i j k ____ m n ____ p q ____ s ____ u ____ w x ____ z

2. A ____ C D ____ F G ____ I ____ K L M ____ O P ____ R ____ T U ____ W ____ Y ____

3.

____ b ____
____ y ____
____ e ____
____ m ____
____ g ____
____ s ____
____ k ____
____ p ____
____ u ____

4.

____ F ____
____ W ____
____ L ____
____ C ____
____ H ____
____ Q ____
____ N ____
____ T ____
____ J ____

A. I need a _____ .

1. quarter   **2.** dime   **3.** nickel   **4.** penny   **5.** dollar
25¢   10¢   5¢   1¢ $1.00

MATCH

quarter $1.00

dime   5¢

penny   10¢

nickel   25¢

dime   1¢

nickel   25¢

quarter   5¢

penny   10¢

dollar   1¢

penny　　　　nickel　　　　dime　　　　quarter

1¢　　　　5¢　　　　10¢　　　　25¢

---

1. How many = ?   _____

2. How many = ?   _____

3. How many = ?   _____

4. How many = ?   _____

5. How many  =  ?   _____

6. How many = ?   _____

7. How many =  ?   _____

8. How many  =  ?   _____

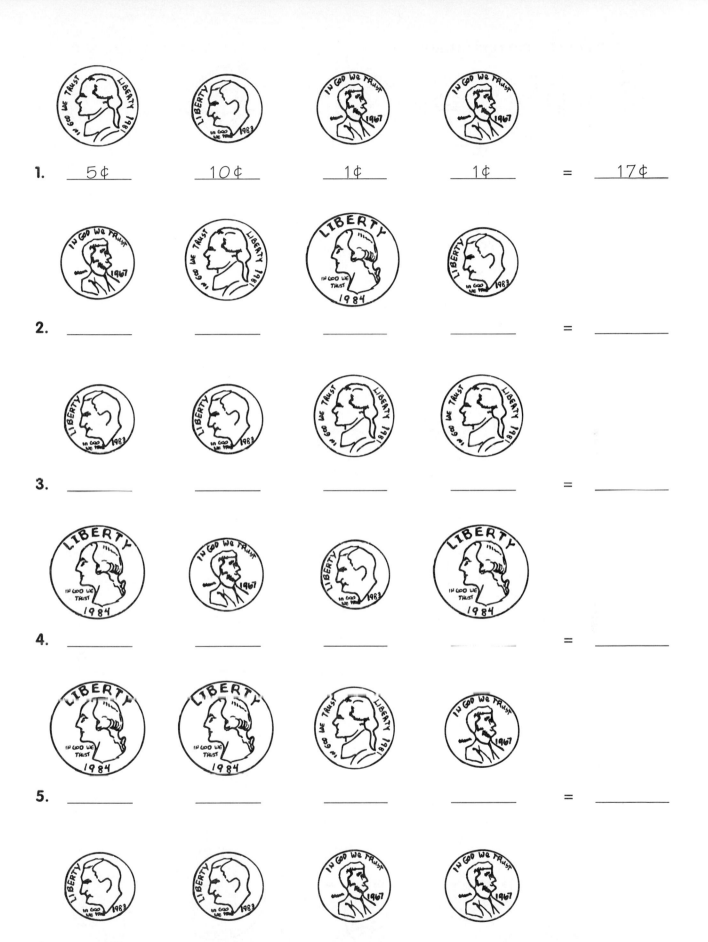

1.   5¢   10¢   1¢   1¢   = 17¢

2. _____   _____   _____   _____   = _____

3. _____   _____   _____   _____   = _____

4. _____   _____   _____   _____   = _____

5. _____   _____   _____   _____   = _____

6. _____   _____   _____   _____   = _____

Circle the correct amount:

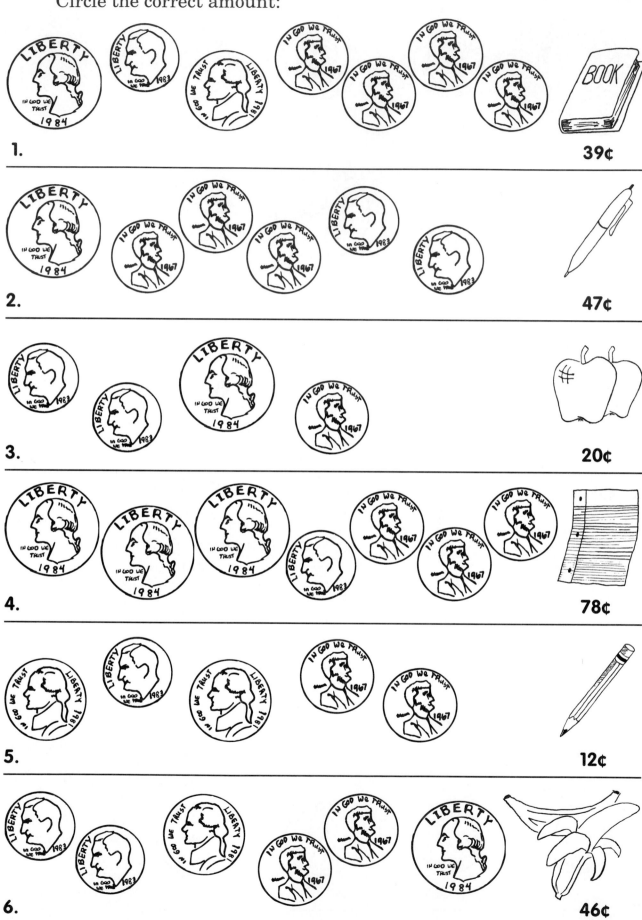

1.   **39¢**

2.   **47¢**

3.   **20¢**

4.   **78¢**

5.   **12¢**

6.   **46¢**

66

3 FAMILY

Essential Vocabulary

. . . .

1.
who's
wife
sister
mother
father
brother
friend
too

2. store

3.
husband
home
doing
taking care of
children
cooking
cleaning
studying
now

4.
doesn't
does
have

how many
has
sons
daughters

5.
do
don't

6.
school
child
one

7.
kindergarten
elementary
grade
teacher
high school
junior high
Mrs.

8.
student
Miss
Mr.
Ms.

9. excited
why
because
coming
parents
grandparents
grandsons
granddaughters
grandchildren

A. Who's she?

B. She's my wife.

A. Is she your sister?

B. No, she isn't. She's my mother.

A. Is he your father?

B. No, he isn't. He's my brother.

A. Is he your brother too?

B. No, he isn't. He's my friend.

mother

brother

friend

wife

husband

wife	husband
sister	brother
mother	father
grandmother	grandfather
aunt	uncle
cousin	cousin
friend	friend

1. My name is _____ .

2. My mother's name is _____ .

3. My father's name is _____ .

4. My grandfather's name is _____ .

5. My grandmother's name is _____ .

6. My sister's name is _____ .

7. My brother's name is _____ .

8. My uncle's name is _____ .

9. My aunt's name is _____ .

10. My friend's name is _____ .

11. My teacher's name is _____ .

State _____

A. Where's your wife?

B. She's at the store.

---

1.  Where's your husband?

_____

2.  Where are your children?

_____

3.  Where's your brother?

_____

A. Where's your husband?

B. He's at home.

A. What's he doing?

B. He's taking care of the children now.

taking care of
cooking

cleaning
studying

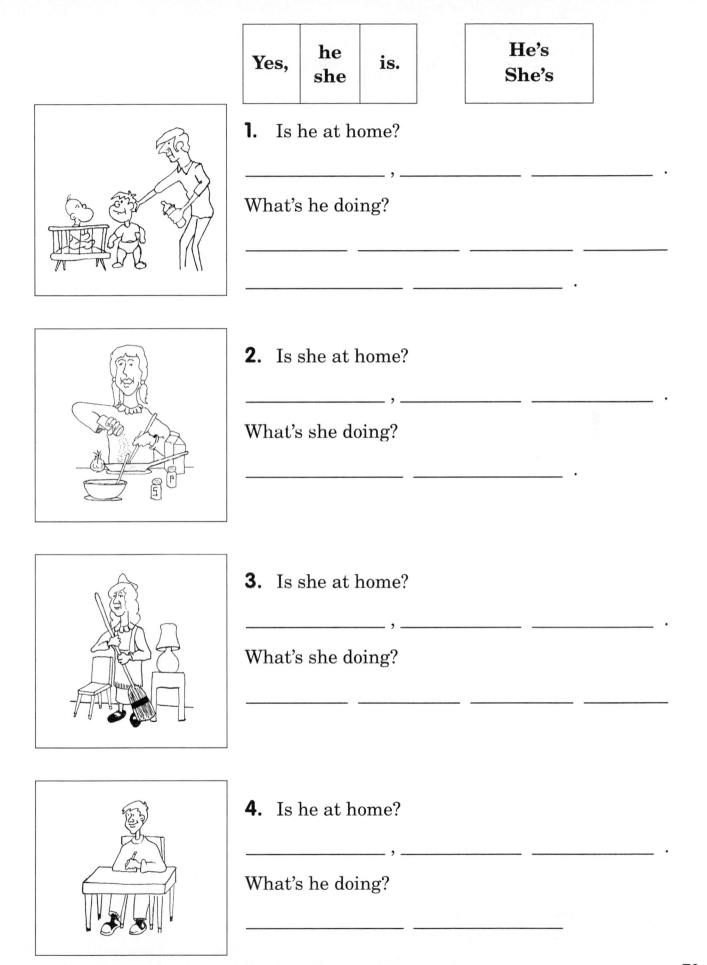

Yes,	he she	is.		He's She's

1. Is he at home?

_____ , _____ _____ .

What's he doing?

_____ _____ _____ _____

_____ _____ .

2. Is she at home?

_____ , _____ _____ .

What's she doing?

_____ _____ .

3. Is she at home?

_____ , _____ _____ .

What's she doing?

_____ _____ _____ _____

4. Is he at home?

_____ , _____ _____ .

What's he doing?

_____ _____

No,	he she	isn't.

1. Is he studying?

No, _____ _____ .

He's _____ _____ _____

_____ _____ .

2. Is she cleaning the house?

No, _____ _____ .

She's _____ .

3. Is he taking care of the children?

No, _____ _____ .

He's _____ .

4. Is she cooking?

No, _____ _____ .

She's _____ .

State _____

A. Does he have children?

B. No, he doesn't.

A. Does she have children?

B. Yes, she does.

A. How many children does she have?

B. She has 5 children.

She has 3 sons and 2 daughters.

Yes,	he she	does.

He She	has

1. Does she have children?

_____ , _____ _____ .

2. How many children does she have?

_____ _____ _____ _____ .

3. Does he have children?

_____ , _____ _____ .

4. How many children does he have?

_____ _____ _____ _____ .

A. Do you have children?

B. No, I don't. I'm single.
   Do you have children?

A. Yes, I do.

B. How many children do you have?

A. I have _____ children.

---

1. Do you have children?

_____ , I _____ .

2. How many children do you have?

I have _____ _____ .

3. Do you have sons?

_____ , I _____ .

4. How many sons do you have?

I have _____ _____ .

5. Do you have daughters?

_____ , I _____ .

6. How many daughters do you have?

I have _____ _____ .

A. Do you have children?

B. Yes, I do.

A. How old are they?

B. One son is 13.

One daughter is 11.

One daughter is 8.

One son is 2.

A. Are they in school?

B. Yes, 3 children are in school.

One child is at home.

Name	How many . . .				
	children	sons	daughters	brothers	sisters

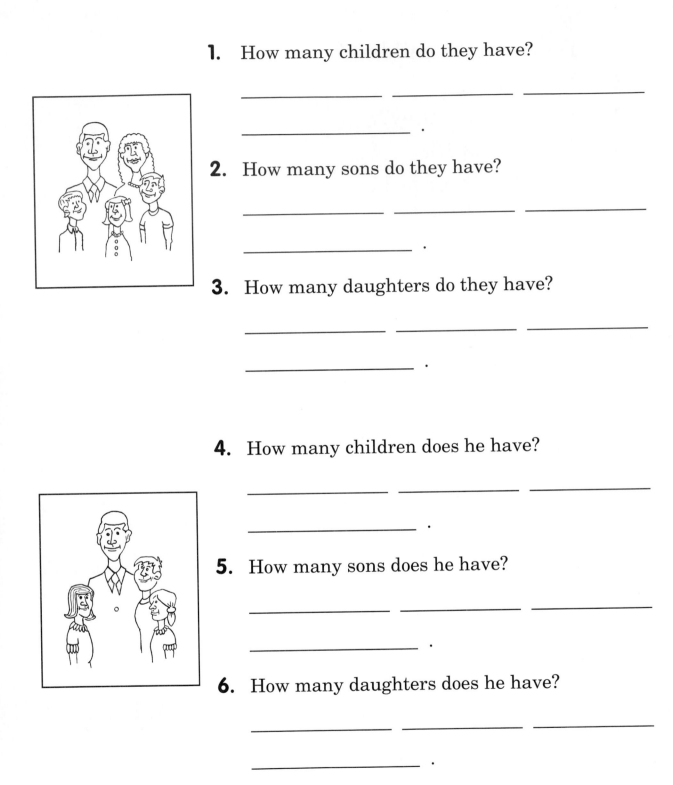

1. How many children do they have?

_____ _____ _____

_____ .

2. How many sons do they have?

_____ _____ _____

_____ .

3. How many daughters do they have?

_____ _____ _____

_____ .

4. How many children does he have?

_____ _____ _____

_____ .

5. How many sons does he have?

_____ _____ _____

_____ .

6. How many daughters does he have?

_____ _____ _____

_____ .

1. How many children does she have?

_____ _____ _____

_____ .

2. How many sons does she have?

_____ _____ _____

_____ .

3. How many daughters does she have?

_____ _____ _____

_____ .

4. How many children do you have?

_____ _____ _____

_____ .

5. How many sons do you have?

_____ _____ _____

_____ .

6. How many daughters do you have?

_____ _____ _____

_____ .

A. Is her son in school?

B. Yes, he is.

A. What school?

B. Bayside Elementary School.

A. What grade?

B. 2nd grade.

A. Who's his teacher?

B. Mrs. Walker.

SCHOOL	AGE
kindergarten	5
1st grade	6
2nd grade	7
3rd grade	8
4th grade	9
5th grade	10
6th grade	11
7th grade	12
8th grade	13
9th grade	14
10th grade	15
11th grade	16
12th grade	17

A. Are you in school?

B. Yes, I am.

A. What school?

B. _____ .

A. Who's your teacher?

B.
| Miss |
| Mr. |
| Mrs. |
| Ms. |
_____

A. Are you a good student?

B. Yes, I am.

_____

1. Are you in school?

_____ , _____ _____ .

2. What school? _____ .

3. Who's your teacher? _____ .

A.   Oh, I'm excited.

B.   Why?

A.   Because my family is coming.

B.   Are your brothers and sisters coming?

A.   Yes, they are.

B.   How many brothers and sisters do you have?

A.   I have 2 brothers and 3 sisters.

B.   Are your parents and grandparents coming, too?

A.   Yes, they are.

B.   I'm excited, too.

1. How many brothers do you have?

_____ _____ _____ _____ .

2. How many sisters do you have?

_____ _____ _____ _____ .

3. How many children do you have?

_____ _____ _____ _____ .

4. How many daughters do you have?

_____ _____ _____ _____ .

5. How many sons do you have?

_____ _____ _____ _____ .

6. How many grandchildren do you have?

_____ _____ _____ _____ .

7. How many granddaughters do you have?

_____ _____ _____ _____ .

8. How many grandsons do you have?

_____ _____ _____ _____ .

Irma is excited.

Her family is coming.

Her 3 brothers and 2 sisters are coming.

Her parents are coming too.

1. Is Irma excited? _____

2. Is her family coming? _____

3. Are her brothers coming? _____

4. Are her sisters coming? _____

5. Is her friend coming? _____

6. Is her father coming? _____

7. Is her mother coming? _____

1. My name is _____ .

2. I'm from _____ .

3. Now I live in _____ .

4. My address is _____ .

5. My zip code is _____ .

6. My telephone number is _____ .

married	divorced
single	widowed

7. I'm _____ .

8. I have _____ children.

9. I have _____ daughters and _____ sons.

10. _____ children are in school.

11. I go to _____ school.

12. My teacher's name is _____ .

13. This is my family.

My Family   See the Teacher's Guide.

Sue and Kim have 4 children.
They have 2 sons and 2 daughters.
3 children are in school.
1 child is at home.

---

1. Do Sue and Kim have children?

_____

2. How many children do they have?

_____

3. Do they have sons?

_____

4. How many sons do they have?

_____

5. Do they have daughters?

_____

6. How many daughters do they have?

_____

7. How many children are in school?

_____

8. How many children are at home?

_____

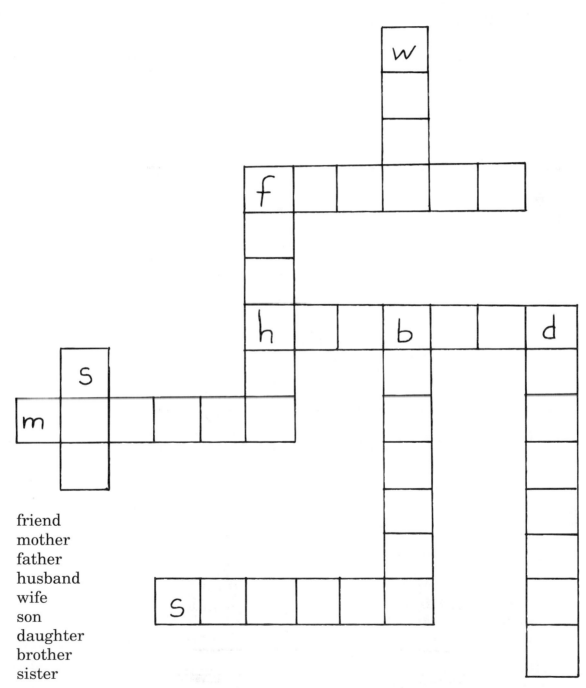

friend
mother
father
husband
wife
son
daughter
brother
sister

4 HEALTH

Essential Vocabulary

....

1. head
eye
nose
chin
back
arm
shoulder
elbow
finger
wrist
foot
toe
hair
ear
mouth
neck
chest
stomach
hand
knee
leg
ankle
body
sick
what's the matter
hurts
hope
feel
better

2. cold
fever
sore throat
a
broken arm

3. this
an
emergency
need
doctor
what's wrong
bleeding

4. let's take
temperature
to see

5. new
patient
fill out
form
sex
male
female

6. hello
let me see
say
cough

some
medicine
here's
prescription
tablet
night
teaspoon
every
hours
drops
capsules

7. Dr. Paul's
office
this
check up
OK
bye

8. coming
dentist
tooth
when
appointment
next

9. hospital
to visit
new
baby
that's wonderful

10. were
had
that's too bad
wrong

THE BODY

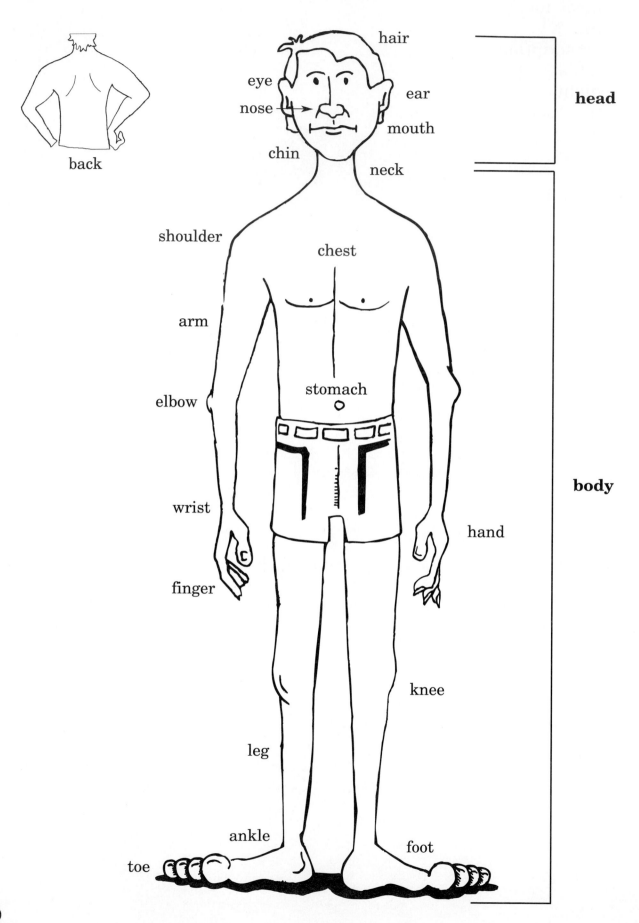

back

hair
eye
nose
ear
mouth
chin
neck

head

shoulder
chest
arm
elbow
stomach
wrist
hand
finger
knee
leg
ankle
foot
toe

body

A. How are you?

B. I'm sick.

A. What's the matter?

B. My stomach hurts.

A. I hope you feel better.

MATCH

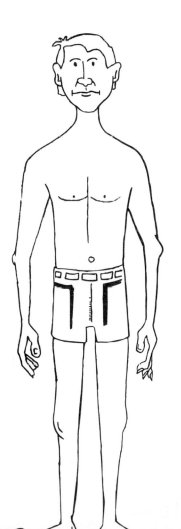

1. eye

2. nose

3. chin

4. back

5. arm

6. elbow

7. finger

8. foot

9. toe

10. body

11. hair

12. ear

13. mouth

14. neck

15. chest

16. stomach

17. hand

18. knee

19. leg

20. head

21. shoulder

WHAT'S THE MATTER?

1. My   _____ _____.

2. My   _____ _____.

3. Her   _____ _____.

4. Her   _____ _____.

5. His   _____ _____.

6. His   _____ _____.

7. Their   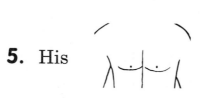   _____s _____.

8. Their   _____s _____.

A.   Do you have a cold?

B.   Yes, I do.

A.   Do you have a fever?

B.   No, I don't.

1.   They have colds.

2.   He has a fever.

3.   He has a broken arm.

4.   She has a sore throat.

No,	he she	doesn't.	He She	has
	I they	don't.	I They	have

1. Does he have a fever?

No, _____ _____ .

He has _____ _____ _____ .

2. Does she have a cold?

No, _____ _____ .

_____ _____ _____ __ _____ _____ .

3. Do they have broken arms?

No, _____ _____ .

_____ _____ _____ _____ .

4. Does he have a sore throat?

No, _____ _____ .

_____ _____ _____ _____ _____ .

5. Do you have a cold?

_____ , I _____ .

6. Do you have a fever?

_____ , I _____ .

7. Do you have a sore throat?

_____ , I _____ .

Lee is sick today.
He has a cold.
He has a sore throat.
He isn't going to school.
He's at home.

1. How is Lee?

   _____.

2. Is he sick?

   _____.

3. What's the matter?

   _____.

4. Does he have a cold?

   _____.

5. Does he have a sore throat?

   _____.

6. Does his stomach hurt?

   _____.

7. Is he going to school?

   _____.

8. Is he at home?

   _____.

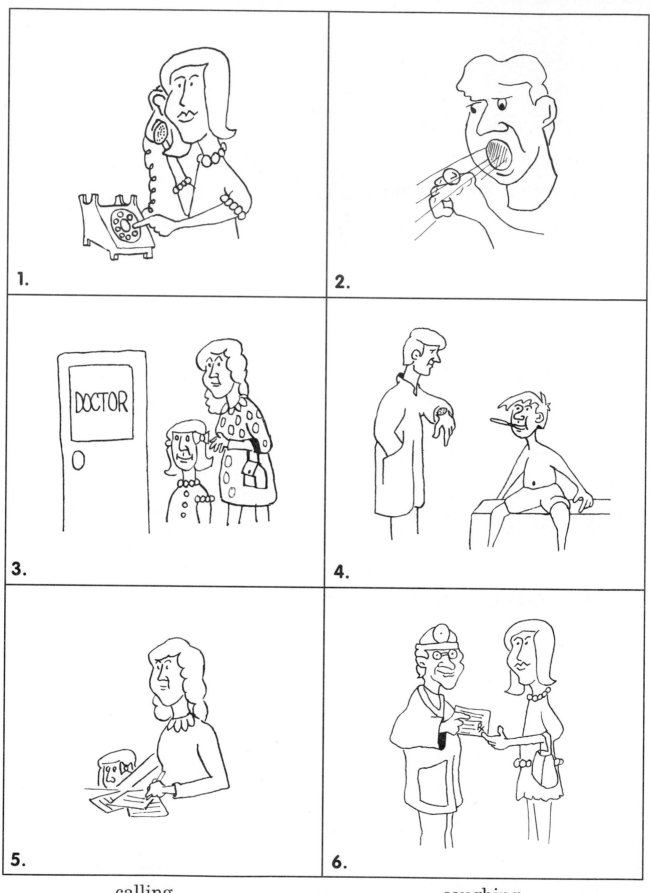

1.
2.
3.
4.
5.
6.

calling
going
filling out

coughing
taking
giving

He's She's	Yes,	he she	is.

1. What's he doing?

_____ _____ .

Is he coughing?

_____ , _____ _____ .

2. What's she doing?

_____ _____ _____ _____ .

Is she calling the doctor?

_____ , _____ _____ .

3. What are they doing?

_____ _____ _____ _____ _____ .

Are they going to the doctor?

_____ , _____ _____ .

4. What's she doing?

_____ _____ _____ _____ _____ .

Is she filling out a form?

_____ , _____ _____ .

5. What's the doctor doing?

_____ _____ _____ _____ .

Is he giving a prescription?

_____ , _____ _____ .

Date _____

911

A. This is an emergency.

I need a doctor.

B. What's wrong?

A. My daughter's head is bleeding.

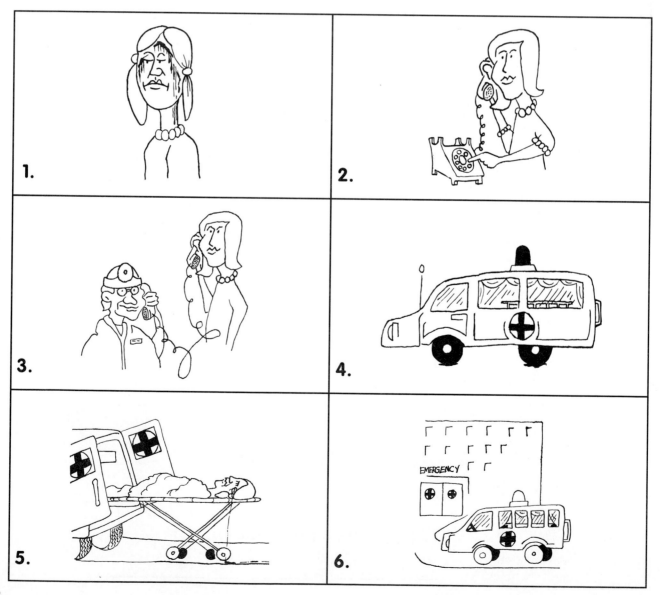

1.

2.

3.

4.

5.

6.

A.   What's wrong?

B.   I have a sore throat.

A.   Let's take your temperature.

      It's 104°.

      You need to see a doctor.

1.   It's 104°.

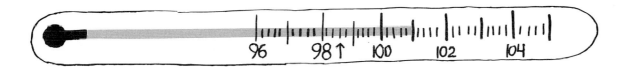

2.   It's _____°.

3.   It's _____°.

4.   It's _____°.

A. Are you a new patient?

B. Yes, I am.

A. Please fill out this form.

Name _____
    last   first

Address _____
    number   street

_____
    city   state   zip code

Phone _____   Age _____

Birthdate _____
        month   day   year

Sex: Male   ☐   Married   ☐   Widowed   ☐
        Female ☐   Single   ☐   Divorced   ☐

A. Hello.

What's the matter today?

B. I have a sore throat.

A. Let me see.

Open your mouth.

Say, "ah."

Cough.

You need some medicine.

Here's a prescription.

1.

2.

3.

Dr. **Lee**

Name _____   Date _____

Address _____

R **X**

_____
doctor's name

1. How much?

_____

When?

_____

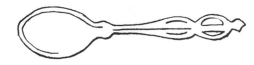

tablespoon

2. How much?

_____

When?

_____

3. How much?

_____

When?

_____

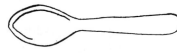

teaspoon

4. How much?

_____

When?

_____

1. How much?

_____

When?

_____

2. How much?

_____

When?

_____

3. How much?

_____

When?

_____

4. How much?

_____

When?

_____

A. Hello.

Dr. Paul's office.

B. Hello.

This is _____ .

My son needs a checkup.

A. What's his name?

B. _____ .

A. O.K. Come in tomorrow at 3:00.

B. Thanks, bye.

| need |
| **needs** |

1. I _____ a checkup.

2. You _____ a checkup.

3. He _____ a checkup.

4. She _____ a checkup.

5. We _____ a checkup.

6. They _____ a checkup.

7. Bob _____ a checkup.

8. Ann _____ a checkup.

WHAT'S THE MATTER?

I	need
he she	needs

1. His head hurts.

He _____ some medicine.

2. Her back hurts.

She _____ some medicine.

3. My stomach hurts.

I _____ some medicine.

medicine

4. My ear hurts.

I _____ some medicine.

5. His chest hurts.

He _____ to see a doctor.

6. Her knee hurts.

She _____ to see a doctor.

doctor

7. My shoulder hurts.

I _____ to see a doctor.

8. My foot hurts.

I _____ to see a doctor.

Telephone number _____

A. Teacher, I'm not coming to school tomorrow.

B. What's wrong?

A. I'm going to the dentist.

B. Does your tooth hurt?

A. No, it doesn't.

   I need a checkup.

B. When is your appointment?

A. At 10:00.

B. O.K.

APPOINTMENT
Ann Lee
Mon. Sep. 18   _10:00 am_
Marlow L. Toms D.D.S.
792-4836

1. What date is the appointment?

_____

2. What time is the appointment?

_____

NEXT APPOINTMENT
Tue. Jan 4   _4:30 p.m._
Bob Jones
Dr. B. E. White
876-6927

3. What date is the appointment?

_____

4. What time is the appointment?

_____

Zip code _____

A. Teacher, I'm not coming to school tomorrow.

B. Why?

A. Because I'm going to the hospital to visit my friend.

B. Is she sick?

A. No, she isn't.
    She has a new baby.

B. That's wonderful.

DRAW A PERSON

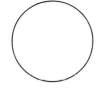

Lila is not coming to school tomorrow.
She is taking her son to the dentist.
Her son has a dentist appointment.
He is not sick.
He has a checkup with the dentist.

---

1. Is Lila coming to school tomorrow?

   _____ .

2. Is her son sick?

   _____ .

3. Does her son have a toothache?

   _____ .

4. Does her son have an appointment?

   _____ .

5. Does her son have a checkup?

   _____ .

6. Where is the appointment?

   _____ .

7. When is the appointment?

   _____ .

8. Why does her son have checkups?

   _____ .

A. Were you sick yesterday?

B. Yes, I was.

A. What was wrong?

B. I had a cold.

A. That's too bad.

Yesterday	I he she	was	sick.
	we you they	were	

Today	I'm he's she's we're you're they're	fine.

FILL IN

1. Yesterday I _____ sick. Today _____ fine.

2. Yesterday he _____ sick. Today _____ fine.

3. Yesterday she _____ sick. Today _____ fine.

4. Yesterday we _____ sick. Today _____ fine.

5. Yesterday you _____ sick. Today _____ fine.

6. Yesterday they _____ sick. Today _____ fine.

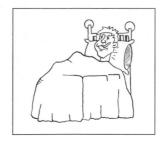

1. Bob is sick.
He has a fever.

2. His mother calls the doctor.

3. Bob and his mother go to the doctor.

4. The nurse takes Bob's temperature.

5. The doctor gives Bob a prescription.

The nurse takes Bob's temperature.

His mother calls the doctor.

Bob is sick. He has a fever.

Bob and his mother go to the doctor.

The doctor gives Bob a prescription.

See the Teacher's Guide.

Yesterday	I you we they he she it	had	medicine.

Today	I you we they	have	medicine.
	he she it	has	

FILL IN

1. Yesterday I _____ a cold.

2. Today I _____ a cough.

3. Yesterday he _____ a toothache.

4. Today he _____ a dentist appointment.

5. Yesterday she _____ a temperature.

6. Now she _____ a headache.

7. I _____ a fever yesterday.

8. Now I _____ some medicine.

9. Yesterday they _____ sore throats.

10. Today they _____ checkups.

Tran was sick yesterday.
He wasn't at school.
He had a sore throat.

---

1. Who was sick yesterday?

_____.

2. Was Tran sick yesterday?

_____.

3. Was Tran at home yesterday?

_____.

4. Was Tran at school yesterday?

_____.

5. What was wrong?

_____.

6. Why was Tran home?

_____.

7. Were you sick yesterday?

_____.

8. Were you at school yesterday?

_____.

9. Were you at home yesterday?

_____.

finger
ear
mouth
stomach
toes
arm
shoulders
back
chest
hair
elbow
nose
foot
head
eye
knee
hand
leg

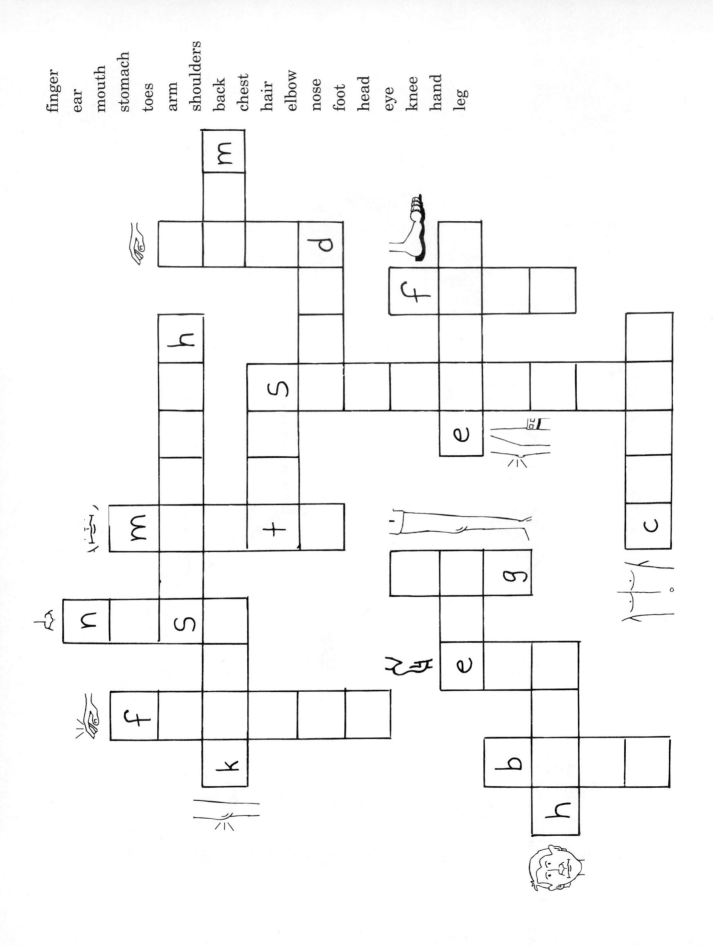

5 TRANSPORTATION

Essential Vocabulary

1. drive
   take
   train
   ride

2. Bus Company
   downtown
   to transfer
   every hour

3. bus stop
   over there
   in front of
   in back of
   next to
   gas station

4. how much
   one way

5. watch your step
   be careful

6. grocery store
   First Street
   on the corner
   pharmacy

7. lost
   shopping center
   turn left
   turn right
   block

8. driver's license
   I'm sorry

9. too fast
   speed limit
   giving
   ticket

10. mechanic
    check
    car
    sure
    engine
    battery
    radiator
    just
    water
    trunk

1.

2.

3.

4.

5.

6.

7.

8.

9.

bicycle motorcycle car / truck
van boat subway
bus airplane train

116

A.   I drive to school.

How do you go to school?

B.   I take the bus.

I drive a

1.

2.

3.

I ride a   to school.

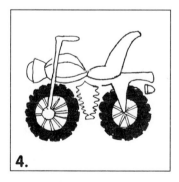

4.

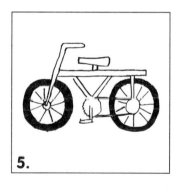

5.

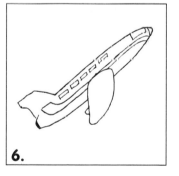

6.

I take the

7.

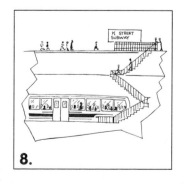

8.

9.

How does $\boxed{\begin{array}{c}\textbf{he}\\\textbf{she}\end{array}}$ go?

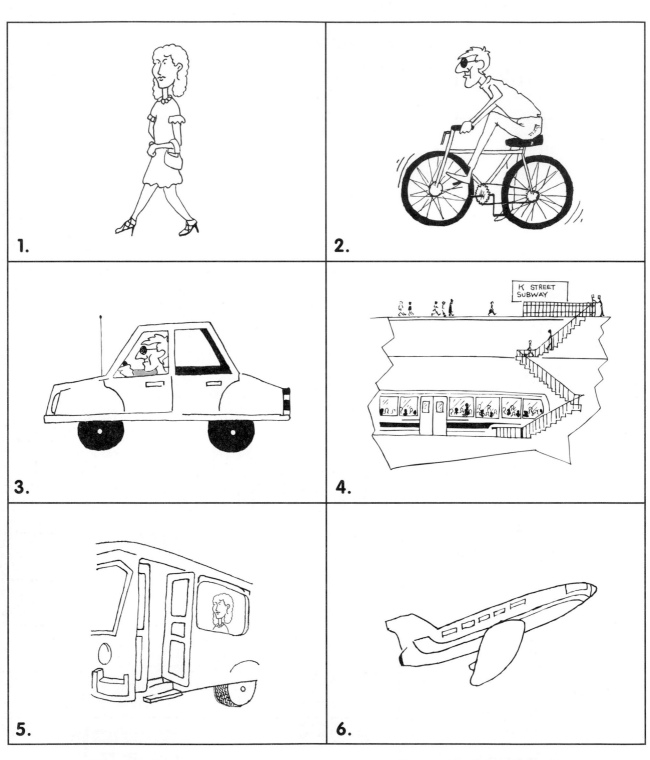

She walks.
He drives his car.
She takes the bus.

He rides his bicycle.
He takes the subway.
She takes an airplane.

1. How does she go to L.A.?

She _____ _____ _____ .

Does she take an airplane?

Yes, _____ _____ .

2. How does he go to L.A.?

He _____ _____ _____ .

Does he drive a car?

Yes, _____ _____ .

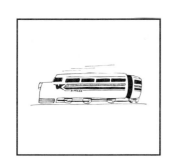

3. How does he go to L.A.?

He _____ _____ _____ .

Does he take the train?

Yes, _____ _____ .

4. How does he go to school?

He _____ _____ _____ .

Does he ride his bicycle?

Yes, _____ _____ .

5. How does she go to school?

She _____ _____ _____ .

Does she take the bus?

Yes, _____ _____ .

6. How does she go to school?

She _____ .

Does she walk to school?

Yes, _____ _____ .

A. Hello, Bus Company.

B. Hello, I'm on _____ Street.
What bus goes downtown?

A. Take the _____ bus.

B. Do I need to transfer?

A. No, you don't.

B. What time does the bus come?

A. Every hour.

B. Thank you. Bye.

A. Bye.

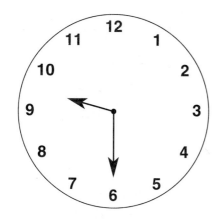

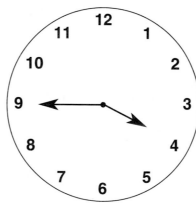

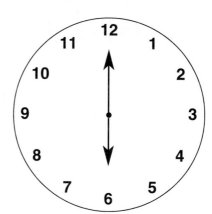

1. It's _____ .   **2.** It's _____ .   **3.** It's _____ .

| Who? | How do they come to school? | How do they go downtown? |
	How does he/she come to school?	How does he/she go downtown?
1.		
2.		
3.		

See the Teacher's Guide.

1.

2. HOSPITAL

3. SCHOOL   105

4. GROCERY STORE

5. 76

6.

7.

8.

9. PHARMACY RX DRUGS

10. SHOP   STORE

11. CINEMA   GONE WITH THE W   NOW PLAYING

12. GAS

downtown	hospital	school
grocery store	home	church / temple
laundromat	park	pharmacy
shopping center	theater	gas station

A. Where's the bus stop?

B. It's over there.

It's | **in front of** | the gas station.
in back of
next to

Match

1. gas station

2. theater

3. grocery store

4. hospital

5. church

6. laundromat

7. pharmacy

8. shopping center

Birth date _____

A. Where are you going?

B. I'm going downtown.

A. Are you taking the bus?

B. Yes, I am.

A. How much is it?

B. _____ one way.

---

1. I'm going  _____ .

2. I'm going to  _____ .

3. I'm going to the  _____ .

A. Is this bus going downtown?

B. Yes, it is. Watch your step. Be careful.

A. Do I need to transfer?

B. No, you don't.

A. Thanks.

Do	I you we they	_____ ?

Does	he she	_____ ?

1. _____ I need to transfer?

2. _____ they need to transfer?

3. _____ we need to transfer?

4. _____ she need to _____ ?

5. _____ he need to _____ ?

6. _____ I need _____ _____ ?

7. _____ you need _____ _____ ?

8. _____ they _____ _____ _____ ?

9. _____ she _____ _____ _____ ?

10. _____ he _____ _____ _____ ?

| Where's the _____ going? |

1. The _____ is going _____ .

 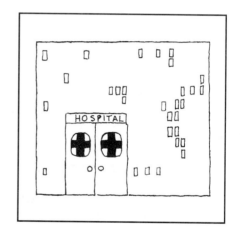

2. The _____ is going to the _____ .

3. The _____ is going to the _____ _____ .

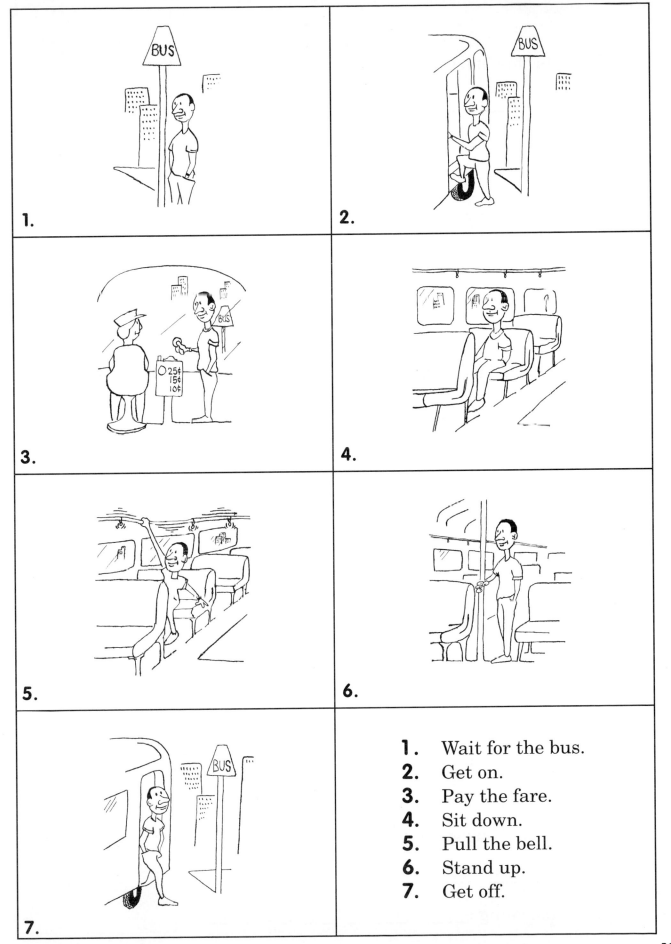

1. Wait for the bus.
2. Get on.
3. Pay the fare.
4. Sit down.
5. Pull the bell.
6. Stand up.
7. Get off.

See the Teacher's Guide.

1. Is this bus going downtown?

_____ , _____ _____ .

2. Is this bus going downtown?

_____ , _____ _____ .

It's going ____ _____ _____ .

3. Is this bus going to the park?

_____ , _____ _____ .

4. Is this bus going to the park?

_____ , _____ _____ .

It's going _____ .

5. Is this bus going to the shopping center?

_____ , _____ _____ .

6. Is this bus going to the hospital?

_____ , _____ _____ .

It's going ____ _____ _____ .

A. Excuse me. Where's the grocery store?

B. It's on First Street.

A. Is it on the corner?

B. No, it isn't. It's next to the pharmacy.

A. Thank you.

Where's the _____ ? It's

next to in front of	the _____ .
on the corner.	
across the street.	

A. I'm lost. Where's the shopping center?

B. Go to A Street and turn right.
Turn left on First Street.
Turn right on B Street.
It's on the corner.

A. Thanks.

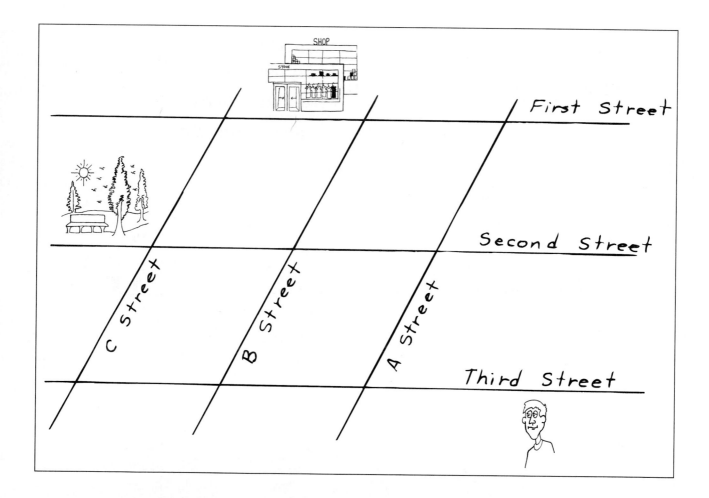

A. Where's the park?

B. Go to _____ Street and turn _____ .
Go one block.
It's on the _____ .

MAP

See the Teacher's Guide.

MAP

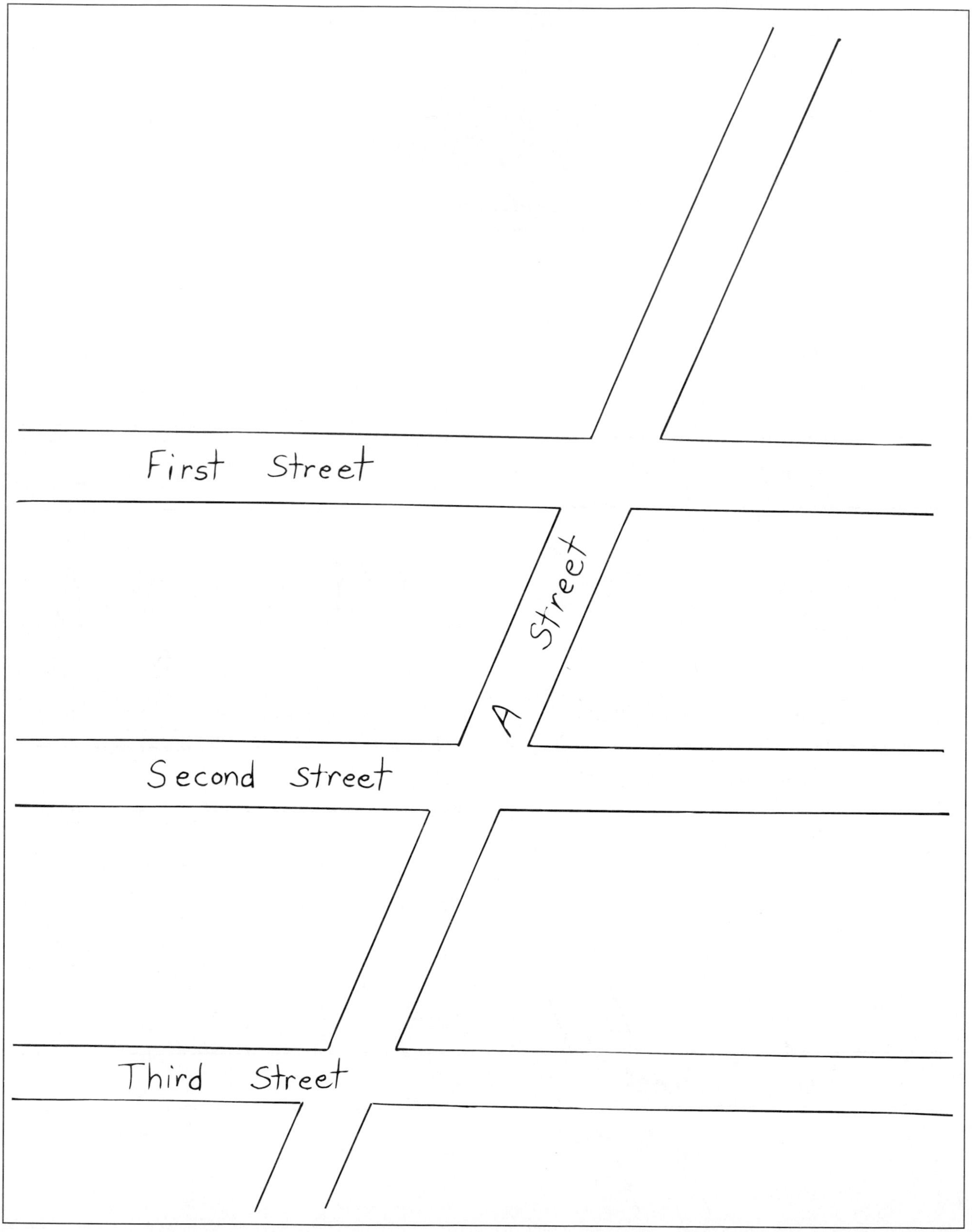

First Street

A Street

Second Street

Third Street

See the Teacher's Guide.

1. Where's the pharmacy?

It's ___ on ___ First ___ Street. ___

Is it on the corner?

_____ , _____ _____ .

2. Where's the laundromat?

It's _____ _____ _____ .

Is it on the corner?

_____ , _____ _____ .

3. Where's the church?

It's _____ _____ _____ .

Is it on the corner?

_____ , _____ _____ .

4. Where's the park?

It's _____ _____ _____ .

Is it on the corner?

_____ , _____ _____ .

5. Where's the grocery store?

It's _____ _____ _____ .

Is it on the corner?

_____ , _____ _____ .

6. Where's the hospital?

It's _____ _____ _____ .

Is it on the corner?

_____ , _____ _____ .

Who?	Where?	How?

1.

2.

3.

See the Teacher's Guide.

A. Do you have a driver's license?

B. No, I don't.

A. That's too bad.

  You need a driver's license.

B. Oh, I'm sorry.

A. Don't drive.

B. Don't drive?

A. Don't drive!

B. O.K.

---

1.  Don't turn left.

2. **NO LEFT TURN** No left turn.

3. **DON'T WALK** Don't walk.
No walking.

4. Don't turn right.

5. **NO RIGHT TURN** No right turn.

6. Don't make a U-turn.

7. **NO U TURN** No U-turn.

Mary is going to a movie.
The theater is downtown.
She takes the #10 bus.
She doesn't need to transfer.
The fare is $1.25 one way.

---

1. Who's going to the movie?

_____

2. Where's Mary going?

_____

3. Where's the theater?

_____

4. Is Mary going to a movie?

_____

5. Is Mary going downtown?

_____

6. Is Mary taking the bus?

_____

7. Is Mary driving a car?

_____

8. What bus goes downtown?

_____

9. How much is the fare one way?

_____

10. How much is the fare round trip?

_____

A.   Do you have a driver's license?

B.   Yes, I do. What's the matter?

A.   You were driving too fast. The speed limit is 55, not 65.

B.   I'm sorry.

A.   I'm giving you a ticket.

SPEED LIMIT **25** MILES **1.**	**STOP** **2.**	ONE WAY ▶ **3.**
▽ YIELD **4.**	DO NOT ⬜ ENTER **5.**	NO PARKING **6.**
SCHOOL CROSSING **7.**	R✕R **8.**	🚶 **9.**

Address _____

A. Are you a mechanic?
B. Yes, I am.

A. Can you check my car?
B. Sure.

A. How's the engine?
B. It's OK.

A. How's the battery?
B. It's OK.

A. How's the radiator?
B. It just needs some water.
A. Oh, good. Thanks.

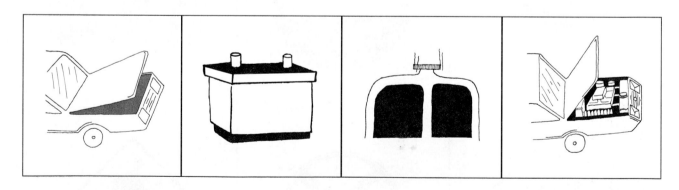

1. _____ 2. _____ 3. _____ 4. _____

1. _____

2. _____

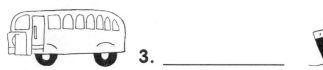

3. _____

4. _____

5. _____

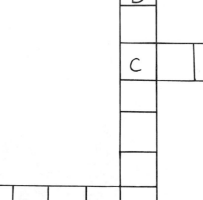

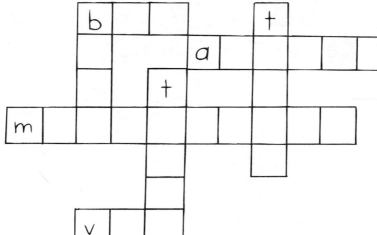

6. _____

7. _____

8. _____

9. _____